The
Connell Short Guide
to

Edward VI

by
Anna Neima

Contents

Introduction

Henry VIII's only legitimate son, Edward, was born on 12 October 1537 at Hampton Court. The king, who had waited 27 years for the arrival of a male heir, wept with joy when he held the newly christened boy. Edward's mother, Henry's third wife Jane Seymour, died soon after, either of puerperal fever or a haemorrhage, after less than two years as queen. Working his way through three more wives, Henry VIII himself died on 28 January 1547, leaving his kingdom in the hands of his nine-year-old son. Edward would reign for only five and a half years, dying on 6 July 1553.

An Ecclesiastes verse was commonly cited at the time: 'Woe unto thee, O land, when thy king is a child'. The accession of a minor presented the potential for catastrophic instability – a possibility that many historians believe Edward VI fully realised. W.R.D. Jones bundles together Henry VIII's declining years, Edward VI's minority and his half-sister Mary's reign as a "mid-Tudor crisis", an aberration of misgovernment in a century of political consolidation. G.R. Elton judges the achievements of the boy-king so paltry that they are given a mere 12 pages in his classic 500-page narrative, *England Under the Tudors*.

Since the 1970s, however, revisionists have reconsidered this near universal indictment. In particular, they have convincingly challenged three central "myths" about Edward's reign. The first of these portrays Edward as an articulate puppet, completely removed from government. The second typecasts Edward Seymour, Lord Protector from 1547 to 1549, as the "good duke" – an idealistic social reformer brought down by a conspiracy of nobles who saw him as a threat to landed interests.* The third dubs Seymour's successor, John Dudley, as the "bad duke" – an unscrupulous, even "psychotic" leader whose only ambition was to acquire and retain power.[1]

In place of these long-established myths, recent biographers have been uncovering evidence that Edward wielded more influence than hitherto thought, and that Seymour and Dudley, rather than being one-dimensional "good" and "bad" dukes, were men of complex political and personal ambitions, each achieving mixed results with their style of rule. Jennifer Loach has been one of several to identify a remarkable overall stability and continuity in government policy, practice and personnel during the Edward years, thereby forcing us to rethink the label "crisis".

Despite reappraisal of Edward's political significance, because of his minority this brief study of his reign is also, inevitably, a study of the rise and fall of his chief councillors, Somerset and Northumberland. It concludes with a look at the

* Edward Seymour was made Earl of Hertford under Henry VIII, and then Duke of Somerset on Henry's death. He is referred to here mainly as Somerset to avoid confusion.

dramatic religious changes of the Edwardian reformation and the legacy of the boy-king.

The education of the boy-king

Edward was given the humanist education Erasmus had prescribed for the ideal Christian prince.[*] He read Aristotle in the original, translated Cicero into Greek, and composed essays on political theory and moral philosophy in French and Latin. Tutors, courtiers and foreign visitors alike praised his precocity, and he seems to have been potentially "the ablest of all the Tudors".[2] Despite his intellectual prowess, many historians have speculated that had he lived longer he would also have been the least attractive ruler of his dynasty. By the time he died, the transition from infant prodigy to a high-handed, dogmatic king looked like a strong possibility.

Edward's lack of personal appeal may lie in his narrow, evangelical indoctrination – although scholars disagree as to how deep this religion actually went. He was tutored by Cambridge-

[*]Desiderius Erasmus (c1466-1536) was a humanist scholar and reformer who believed strongly in humanity's capacity for self-improvement through education. He had a huge influence on the generation that came of age under Henry VIII, including Edward's tutors and Thomas Cranmer.

educated humanists, including Roger Ascham, Roger Cox and John Cheke, all of whom demonstrated a zealous commitment to radical reform. These evangelicals assiduously promoted the idea of the monarch's fervent piety, in part to counteract anxiety about his youth but also to safeguard the religious reforms instituted by his father. They compared him to Josiah of the Old Testament, who purged his land of idols, and to King Solomon, son of David, who rebuilt the Temple of Jerusalem. The abiding image of the young king is a 1563 woodcut included in the Protestant hagiographer John Foxe's *Acts and Monuments*, which depicts him devoutly listening to a Lenten sermon given by Hugh Latimer (a bishop infamous for his fierce sermons who was later martyred for his faith under Queen Mary).

How valid and comprehensive is this image? The "Chronicle", a journal of foreign and domestic events kept by Edward throughout his reign, frequently mentions masques and jousts, but never sermons. For Jennifer Loach this "casts doubt on the depth of his supposed zeal". But it is known that the king also noted down court sermons in a separate ledger, now lost, and Diarmaid MacCulloch has drawn attention to the zeal and theological competence of Edward's surviving writings on religion – for example, a remarkable treatise against papal supremacy written in 1549. Many of his acts, such as repeatedly rebuking his

The Family of Henry VIII c. 1545 depicting (L-R) Mary I, Edward VI, King Henry VIII, Jane Seymour and Elizabeth I

half-sister Mary for her adherence to the Catholic Mass, or insisting on the removal of references to the saints in the oath of supremacy, could well be ascribed to a godly youth – but they could equally be attributed to a young king's impatience to have his regal will obeyed.

However accurate the conventional view of Edward's piety, what is certainly inaccurate is the traditional view of him as permanently sickly and studious. Until the final months of his life, he participated in the lavish rituals of a rich, cosmopolitan Renaissance court just like any other young nobleman. He was interested in fine clothes, jewels, court ceremony, sports and all things military. An observer noted him "arming and tilting, managing horses and delighting in every sort of exercise, drawing the bow, playing rackets, hunting and so forth, indefatigably, though he never neglected his studies" – hardly a portrait of a sickly individual. His journal is full of mentions of military manoeuvres and he copied out copious notes about Henry VI's military occupation of Normandy. Ultimately, as Catherine Davies remarks, "chivalry and piety are not mutually exclusive".

How much power did Edward wield?

Scholars have generally been unimpressed by Edward VI's political significance. Edward "was obviously too young to rule", writes Jennifer Loach: "the history of his reign must therefore be the history of those who ruled in his name". For G.R. Elton, his "character and views matter little". His "so-called opinions were those of his advisers and his so-called acts were his endorsements of accomplished fact".

There is no doubt that under the Duke of Somerset, Edward was sidelined. The Lord Protector, ruling as a "quasi-king", largely ignored the young monarch except for ceremonial purposes.[3] This was a mistake he may well have regretted when, at the time of his fall, rebels upset his rule and Edward was readily convinced by other councillors of his guilt and made no plea for the preservation of his life.

The Duke of Northumberland was subtler in his methods. When he took over the king was 12 and would soon achieve his majority; Northumberland knew that he risked losing power and favour if his actions were out of tune with Edward's wishes. In consequence he took great pains with Edward's political education: from August 1551 onwards he ensured that Edward regularly attended council meetings, and from May 1552 the king was directly participating in everyday financial affairs.

By his teenage years Edward was "an exceptionally capable student of state affairs" – his Chronicle demonstrates a precocious grasp of a vast range of political matters, from trade and debasement of coinage to the diplomatic intricacies of monarchical marriage.[4] In the latter part of his reign he increasingly initiated and adjudicated decision-making. He wrote a host of letters to key figures in the court and council and, between 1551 and his death, composed 17 state papers, some of which were read out at council meetings. Such was his grasp of affairs – Diarmaid MacCulloch calls him "a Henry VIII in the making" – that it was agreed to lower the age of his majority from 18 to 16. He would have taken formal control of his government in October 1554. All this has persuaded some historians that Edward was wielding power and influencing politics, regardless of the fact he was so young.

Nonetheless, Edward's apparently dynamic role at court was, in part, smoke and mirrors. Northumberland radiated unusual force of character and quickly won the king's trust and admiration. As Dale Hoak observes, he could then afford to allow Edward's exercise of power in more peripheral matters, giving the impression that he was governing "as a king counseled" while in reality much of the king's thinking was being done for him. Northumberland's adroit technique was noted by one French visitor: "he visited the King secretly at night in the King's chamber . . . The next day the young Prince came to his council and proposed matters as if they were his own; consequently, everyone was amazed."

Does Somerset deserve his reputation as the "good duke"?

Edward Seymour (c1500-1553) was the second of ten children of a prominent courtier and educated at Oxford and Cambridge. His steady rise up through Henry VIII's court was boosted by his sister Jane's marriage to the king, and her subsequent production of a male heir. Few were surprised that Seymour was named as one of the 16 executors of Henry's will.

The executors were supposed to form a regency council to govern the country collectively until Edward's majority (his 18th birthday), but even before Henry VIII's death Somerset had planned to subvert this arrangement. He plotted with Henry's secretary, Sir William Paget, to secure the other executors' support by promising them titles, commissions and lands. They appointed him Lord Protector of the Realm and Governor of the King's Person. Although this initially required him to govern with their consent, a patent dated 12 March 1547 widened his remit, allowing him, in effect, to act alone, and thus giving him more power than any other subject since the beginning of Tudor rule.

For a long time historians lauded Somerset as the "good duke". A.F. Pollard portrayed an idealistic, liberal leader, out to defend constitutional freedom, Protestantism and the poor. In the 1970s, however, this romanticised interpretation came under attack from M.L. Bush, among others, who probed Somerset's motives more closely and concluded that his "political behaviour was directed not by ideals, but by idées fixes". He was especially criticised for his grandiose obsession with pursuing a destructive Scottish war that would eventually bring down his government.

Was Somerset a true social reformer?

Somerset indubitably took certain humanitarian steps and many historians see him as a thoroughgoing social radical. He repealed Henry VIII's harsh treason legislation, and was the first to prohibit the custom of duelling "whose motive is vainglory rather than justice". He seems to have been genuinely averse to excessive cruelty or violence – as shown by his marked reluctance to do away with his political opponents, or to use violence to quell rebellion.

Nonetheless, many of the Protector's broader measures for social reform were executed with an inconsistency that may, as C.S.L. Davies would have it, indicate "sheer incompetence", but could also suggest that his heart was not entirely in the project. M.L. Bush has convincingly surmised that his liberalism was, to some extent, a pose adopted to bolster his unstable position as Protector: lacking the bulwark of the "divinely sanctioned" authority that kings could rely on, he courted popularity instead. While Somerset's sympathy with the grievances of the commoners may well have been genuine, he was ultimately keener to defend the natural order (which included his own and the king's supremacy) than to reform it.

This inconsistency is most evident in his measures against enclosure. The first half of the century had seen a rapid growth in the cloth trade, resulting in huge demand for wool. Wanting a greater share in the trade, landlords began expanding their grazing by converting arable land to pasture and enclosing the common land traditionally used by villagers. This was bitterly resented and many pamphlets were written against the practice. In response, Somerset issued two proclamations against enclosure, established a commission to investigate malefactors, and tried to limit the number of sheep by imposing a poll tax on them. Yet his proclamations promised more than they delivered, the commission did little to slow the process of enclosure, and the poll tax was repealed after just eight months. A key reason for Somerset's fall was that he raised unrealistic hopes of liberal reform among the poor, and their subsequent disappointment led them to rebel.

A further measure that belies Somerset's image as a "friend of the poor" is his draconian Vagrancy Act (1547). This unprecedentedly ferocious legislation entailed threats of branding and slavery for the work-shy. It was repealed in 1549, in large part due to its unenforceability.

Why would a "good duke" have his brother executed?

Thomas Seymour, Somerset's brother, was described by Hugh Latimer as "a man furthest from the fear of God that ever I heard or knew of in

England". Attractive, charming and hugely ambitious, he gathered in offices, rewards and commissions as the Seymour family rose under Henry. But although he was ennobled and appointed as Lord High Admiral when his brother became Lord Protector, Thomas was dissatisfied with his position in the new regime – he thought he should, at the very least, be Governor of the King's Person.

In revenge, and in defiance of his brother, he married Henry VIII's widow, Katherine Parr (whom he had earlier courted before she caught the king's eye). Following her death in September 1548, he began a reckless bid to secure the hand of the 15-year-old Princess Elizabeth instead, and to gain influence over the king by passing him notes and pocket money, telling him "Ye are a beggarly king, ye have no money to play or to give". He also tried to recruit various noblemen to his side in an effort to gain a more solid power base.

His brother Somerset was for a long time forbearing – which has contributed to the "good duke" image – but the final straw came when Thomas Seymour manipulated the Bristol mint into producing false coinage to spend on weapons. Declaring "how sorowfull a case this was unto hym", Somerset arranged in January 1549 for his attainder in parliament and subsequent beheading. According to G.W. Bernard, there was no "fratricidal bitterness" involved: Somerset had, ultimately, to regard his duty to the king over his loyalty to his brother, and he had the support of his fellow privy councillors.

Why was Somerset's foreign policy so damaging?

In his final years Henry VIII was obsessed with forging "the empire of greate Briteigne" through a union of England and Scotland. After making war on Scotland for several years, a period known as the "Rough Wooing", he succeeded in negotiating the Treaty of Greenwich (1543), by which the infant Edward was betrothed to seven-month-old Mary, Queen of Scots. The betrothal was short-lived, and the breakdown of the Treaty led to more years of inconclusive strife, which continued – with several French interventions on the side of the Scots – right up to Henry's death.

Somerset was involved in these campaigns as a diplomat rather than as a soldier. Once installed as Lord Protector, he was determined to finish where Henry had left off. At first he tried to revive the Treaty of Greenwich. When this failed (Mary's mother was pro-French), he invaded Scotland with 18,000 men. The resulting Battle of Pinkie, just east of Edinburgh on 10 September 1547, was an overwhelming victory for the English – but the triumph proved hollow. The French quickly sent a force of 6,000 to help the Scots attack Somerset's garrisons. Mary was betrothed to the dauphin, François, instead of to Edward, and soon departed for France. At the same time, fighting broke out on the Continent, with the French determined to wrest Calais and Boulogne back from English control.

War on two fronts was vastly expensive, particularly because Somerset relied heavily on highly paid mercenaries. He tried to cover the cost with a tax on sheep and the sale of ecclesiastical property. Twice in his 33 months in power, he debased the coinage: the currency was melted down and new coinage was issued with a lower silver content, leaving the crown with leftover silver to spend. It was a quick way of obtaining money, but it was unsustainable, creating distrust and fuelling inflation. Even with this measure, finances fell critically short of what was needed. By September 1549 the crown was nearly bankrupt.

The 1549 rebellions and Somerset's fall

As conditions worsened, the Lord Protector grew increasingly autocratic and unresponsive to advice. His high-handed style was made manifest in an extensive use of proclamations: over the 33 months of his Protectorate he issued 76, a higher rate than in any other such period in the century. Privy council meetings were effectively a sham. Somerset was often recorded as having attended them when he was actually out of London; his signature was added to documents later. Dale Hoak writes that his "near-abandonment" of the council brought the government "close to ruin".

This over-personal style of rule aroused deep resentment both in the council and outside it. His growing unpopularity was compounded by the major financial difficulties already apparent in summer of 1548. Despite this, Protector Somerset was still determined to succeed in Scotland. He tried to mobilise troops for a renewed campaign, but then, in spring 1549, rebellions, riots and disorder forced him to abandon the attempt.

From April to August 1549, domestic unrest engulfed about fifteen counties, plunging England into the century's "greatest crisis".[5] This disturbance arose from a mixture of economic, social and religious grievances. The largest risings occurred in the southwest and in East Anglia. In Devon and Cornwall opposition to the new Book of Common Prayer turned into a full scale "western rising", with rebels, often abetted by their local clergy, marching toward London. They were stopped by a failed siege of Exeter.

In East Anglia, where the rebels settled down in camps rather than advancing on London, motives were more various. An early socialist historian celebrated Robert Kett, the leader of the longest surviving rebel camp at Mousehold, close to Norwich, for his "hatred of mastery and thraldom and his love of equality and brotherhood".[6] Subsequent left-leaning scholars took this further – Andy Wood asserting that "commoner" insurgency, driven by proto-Marxist resistance to agrarian capitalism, was part of the long-term formation of the working class. Jennifer Loach, however, demonstrates that many rebel leaders, far from being commoners, ranked just below the gentry. Robert Kett, for instance, was a prosperous tanner. Another leader, John Harbottle, was a lesser merchant who owned two manors. Such men had been alienated from their immediate social superiors and were "seeking good government" from the crown.[7] Kett formed an elected council who sent details of their demands to the king.

The Lord Protector was slow to react to this crisis. Diarmaid MacCulloch attributes this to his sympathy with the rebels' grievances; Barrett L. Beer sees it as just as much the result of poor communication about the seriousness of the revolt. Eventually, nine letters were written at Somerset's behest to the various gatherings of rebels. He promised to receive petitions, grant pardons, make concessions and plan further reform. The negotiations failed, however, and he resorted to military force – though he had to wait for troops recalled from the Scottish border.

In what was a fateful move, Somerset called on John Dudley (soon to be Duke of Northumberland), to quell Kett's East Anglian rebellion. Dudley did so systematically, killing at least 2,000 rebels. He then returned to the capital, but did not disband his troops. His attitude to the Protector seems to have undergone a radical change – possibly due to Somerset's incompetence in managing the insurgency. Where previously he had worked with him in harmony, he now joined a group of leading conservative peers to plot Somerset's overthrow. Fed up with being ignored and knowing they had Northumberland's troops behind them, most of the privy council supported their conspiracy.

Somerset was with the king at Hampton Court when news reached him of the conspiracy, and he immediately sent out a general appeal for assistance. Thousands of men gathered, but they lacked military training. Archbishop Thomas Cranmer and Somerset's long-standing ally Sir William Paget were two of the handful of councillors to rally to the Protector's side – although Cranmer's intention may well have been to defuse the situation and defend the reformation. Somerset, knowing himself outmanoeuvred, retreated with Edward to the more secure Windsor Castle, and after a tense stand-off, surrendered.

Somerset was imprisoned and the Protectorate was dissolved on 13 October 1549. For a few months the privy council assumed collective responsibility for government, but John Dudley soon emerged as leader. He was never formally appointed Protector, but became the king's leading minister. In February 1550 he secured Edward's approval for his appointment to the offices of Great Master and Lord President. The former gave him control of the king's household; the latter enabled him to supervise the council.

Some have alleged that Northumberland had been planning Somerset's ruin all along – A.F. Pollard labelled him the "subtlest intriguer in history". He was even said to have encouraged Thomas Seymour's earlier conspiracies, but there is little evidence to support this theory. Rather, he seems until close to the end to have been a trusted ally – significantly he played a distinguished role at the Battle of Pinkie, for which he received £100-worth of land in gratitude from the Protector. Many petitioners, seeking Somerset's ear, first approached Northumberland because of his presumed influence with him. It is most likely that it was only the dire circumstances of 1549, and Somerset's clear inability to deal with the crisis, that led Northumberland on his path to influence.

Is it fair to call Northumberland the "bad duke"?

The son of an executed traitor, John Dudley was brought up and launched on a successful career as a courtier and soldier by his guardian, Sir Edward Guildford.* Dudley married Guildford's daughter and, after the premature death of Guilford's own son, received from him a substantial inheritance. Like Somerset, he distinguished himself markedly in the last years of Henry VIII's reign, first administering the Scottish borders, then overhauling the navy as Lord High Admiral, and finally helping negotiate peace with France. The far-sighted Imperial Ambassador, Eustace Chapuys, predicted that in the case of Henry's death Dudley and Somerset would have "the management of affairs, because, apart from the King's affection for them, and other reasons, there are no other nobles of a fit age and ability for the task".

In spite of this, historians have given Dudley a bad press. He was, according to Barrett L. Beer, "distinguished neither by learning, administrative

---

* Northumberland's father, Edmund Dudley, was a highly trusted servant of Henry VII who helped him establish the Tudor monarchy on a sound financial basis. The king's death led to Dudley's execution in 1510, with all his property being forfeit to the crown.

talent, nor political genius". In the view of W.K. Jordan, he was a ruthless and "psychotic" intriguer who brought England near to ruin with his "obsessive fears" of popular disorder. His emergence as the most powerful man in England in 1549 was "one of the most unlikely events of the Tudor century".[8] Where Somerset, the "friend of the poor", fell because of his excessive populism, Northumberland –self-aggrandising, cold and ruthless – was said to have died "one of the least beloved figures in English history".[9]

Since the 1970s, revisionists have reassessed both the man and his priorities. David Loades's biography suggests that Northumberland should be understood not as a magnate in the traditional mould but as a businessman and politician – one of a pioneering breed of "service nobility" – who saw himself "first and foremost as a servant of the crown". While he might have lacked spiritual or intellectual depth, he showed great ability in co-ordinating greater minds and in pursuing his political strategy "to reduce the king's debts, to consolidate his position as supreme head of the church, and to reinforce the privy council's administrative machinery".[10]

Reducing the crown's debts

Northumberland inherited from Somerset a calamitous financial situation: by 1550 the crown was £300,000 in debt and inflation had risen by about 75 per cent in two years. War continued with both France and Scotland. Facing crisis, he dropped Somerset's aggressive Scottish policy and negotiated a peace treaty with France. This included the surrender of Boulogne, triumphantly acquired with much bloodshed by Henry VIII in 1544. The historian A.F. Pollard called the Treaty of Boulogne "the most ignominious" to be signed by England during the century. However, Edward's Chronicle records general rejoicing when peace was declared. Boulogne had swallowed up resources out of all proportion to its strategic value; its sale allowed Northumberland to redeploy its garrison to improve domestic security, and to use the money to pay off some of the crown's debts.

Northumberland also attempted to restore the coinage after multiple debasements under Henry VIII and Somerset. This scheme was ultimately successful, if poorly managed: he announced his intention in advance, leading to a general loss of confidence that nearly amounted to a complete fiscal breakdown in May 1552. The situation was retrieved, however, in large part due to the enormously profitable activity of Sir Thomas Gresham, who had been appointed by Northumberland as the king's agent on the

Antwerp exchange.* The restoration of the currency was an incredible achievement and, by the end of 1553, almost all of the crown's debt had been repaid.

Reinforcing the governing class

In his style of rule, Northumberland was far more ready to delegate than Somerset. In Barrett L. Beer's view "he personally supplied few of the ideas" for government, but "lent his authority and gave encouragement to the experts". While this might sound like a negative trait, it was in fact a sign of the effective restoration of a conciliar government, which Dale Hoak thinks was "Northumberland's main service to the crown". Hoak's study of the Edwardian council shows that while Somerset increasingly circumvented his council, Northumberland set out to create one that was strong enough to take decisions even in his absence, but which he could still control and manage. In doing so he made the council a principle instrument of monarchical government, a position that it retained to the end of the Tudor period.

Northumberland also pursued unity where he

* Sir Thomas Gresham was a remarkably successful textile dealer and merchant adventurer who acted on-and-off as the crown's financial agent in the Netherlands exchange under Edward, Mary and Elizabeth. He also founded both the Royal Exchange, modeled on the Antwerp bourse, and Gresham College, the first institution of higher learning in London.

could. In February 1550 he ordered Somerset's release from prison, and in April readmitted him to the privy council. In a grand gesture of public reconciliation he married one of his many sons to Somerset's daughter, Anne. Unfortunately Somerset was not prepared to take his relegation with a good grace. He made his disaffection with Northumberland's policies obvious, intriguing with other of the Lord President's opponents. Deciding that the danger of a split in the ruling elite was too grave to be ignored, on 22 January 1552 Northumberland had Somerset executed for felony.[*]

Outside the privy council, Northumberland also judged that the unity of the ruling class was the key priority – although several of his actions also promoted social justice. He repealed Somerset's savage Vagrancy Act; passed legislation that helped homeless cottagers find accommodation; and his anti-enclosure policies, although less spectacular than Somerset's, were more effective in ensuring prosecutions. But he mainly concentrated on shoring up the nobles and gentry, distributing favours and rewards with a generous hand. The policy worked: they enforced his rule and order was maintained. David Loades writes that, unlike under Somerset, the governing class

[*] Somerset successfully argued his way out of charges of treason, but he was convicted of felony (i.e. a serious crime) for having assembled an illegal force – an offence of which he was probably guilty.

FIVE FACTS ABOUT
KING EDWARD VI

1.

The new-born prince was named Edward, after his great-grandfather and because he was born on the eve of the Feast of St Edward. Upon his birth, 2,000 shots were fired from the Tower of London.

2.

Edward VI was the inspiration for the central character in Mark Twain's novel *The Prince and The Pauper* in which Edward and Tom Canty, a pauper, swap places.

3.

At his accession, Edward inherited 55 palaces, more than any other monarch in Europe.

4.

Concerned for Edward's security and health, his father issued obsessively detailed instructions for the hygienic conditions of his residences and hand-picked the officers of his household.

5.

The personal motto of Edward was *Idem per Diversa* which translates as 'The same, no matter the circumstances'.

Opposite: Edward as Prince of Wales, 1546 by an artist of the Flemish school

"spoke with a single voice". Northumberland was probably helped in keeping the lid on discontent by the severe outbreak of "sweating sickness" in 1551 and 1552, alongside his introduction of fairly stringent penalties for subversion.

Who designed the "Devise for the Succession"?

The final act of Northumberland's career, and the one for which he is mainly remembered, was his attempt to divert the succession from Edward's half-sister Mary to Lady Jane Grey. The failure of the king's health from early in 1553 was a crushing blow to Northumberland. Initially, Edward was expected to recover, but by May it was clear that his sickness – probably pulmonary tuberculosis – was likely to be mortal. The king signed a "Devise for the Succession" in favour of the male heirs of Lady Jane Grey and of her sisters, Catherine, Mary and Eleanor. As no children had yet been born, the devise was hurriedly altered to include Lady Jane herself when it was realised how close to death Edward was.

The most commonly held view, and one of the main reasons for Northumberland's vilification over the subsequent centuries, is that in "an act of futile desperation" he bullied the dying boy to alter the succession.[11] Some historians have even suggested – though with little plausibility or evidence – that he poisoned the king, thinking Lady Jane would be easier to manipulate. Northumberland certainly had little to hope from a Catholic Queen Mary: he could expect only loss of office, imprisonment, and possible execution. One key fact supports the argument that Northumberland forced the king's hand: Lady Jane Grey married Northumberland's son Guildford on 21 May 1553.

The limitation of surviving sources makes it impossible absolutely to disprove this theory. There is, however, much circumstantial evidence against it: Jane had not been the duke's first choice for his son, and when Edward's law officers demurred at the breach of Henry's statute of succession, it was Edward himself "with sharp words and angry countenance" who commanded them to obey him. What is more, Edward regarded Jane as his spiritual sister: she had absorbed the same "godly learning" of the evangelic reformers, and could be trusted to carry forward his reformation.

When Edward died on 6 July 1553, Northumberland stuck to the devise and made Jane queen. What he was trying to do was widely regarded as unlawful, and most people – from commoners to councillors – declared for Mary rather than Jane. On 23 July, by which time the majority of his troops had deserted,

Northumberland surrendered and was imprisoned in the Tower of London. Convicted of high treason, his appeals for clemency fell on deaf ears and on 22 August Mary had him executed on Tower Hill.[*]

Who was responsible for the Edwardian religious reformation?

Between 1547 and 1553 the ecclesiastical compromises of the late Henrician church gave way to full-blown Protestant evangelism. Many of the visible religious changes came early: churches were whitewashed and their images and ornaments removed; the veneration of the saints was forbidden; chantries were dissolved along with colleges and religious guilds; the imposition of celibacy on the clergy was ended.[**] More significant still was English becoming the language

[*] Northumberland's son, Robert Dudley, Earl of Leicester, lived on to become Elizabeth I's great favourite and, for a time, was viewed as a potential husband for her.

[**] A chantry is an endowment for the saying of Masses and prayers for the soul of the endower. Catholics believed that this would speed the soul's journey through purgatory to heaven. Chantry chapels, set aside for this purpose, often accumulated huge wealth. As purgatory did not feature in reformed Protestantism, these endowments proved rich pickings for the crown. Some of the chantries were converted into schools named after the king, hence the large number of Edward VI grammar schools.

Edward VI and the Pope: An Allegory of the Reformation., *1575*

of religious services. A new liturgy in English, the
first Book of Common Prayer, was issued in March
1549.

The driving force behind these changes was
Archbishop Thomas Cranmer. Under Henry VIII
his fortunes had been mixed, but he had enjoyed a
close relationship with Somerset and Edward's
tutors: Ascham, Cox and Cheke. He also had
forged strong links with leading Continental
reformers such as Martin Bucer at Strasbourg, and
from the beginning of the Edwardian regime he
sought to push England to the forefront of the
international Protestant reformation.

What Somerset himself thought about this
reform is difficult to judge. He had a warm

relationship with leading evangelicals, including Cranmer, but Jennifer Loach sees his interest in reform as mainly motivated by the chance to consolidate the royal supremacy and his own personal assets, which swelled considerably with the dissolution of church property.

Under Northumberland, the pace of the move to reformist Protestantism accelerated further. A second, more radical Prayer Book was introduced in 1552, explicitly rejecting the Catholic doctrine of transubstantiation.* It is this that remains, with some Elizabethan amendments, at the heart of Anglican liturgy today. In June 1553, the 42 Articles were issued, a declaration that included the Protestant doctrine of justification by faith and a denial of the Catholic doctrine of purgatory. ** These, modified as the 39 Articles in 1563, have also remained doctrinally central to the Church of England.

Again, historians dispute how deeply Northumberland believed in this radical reform. Chris Skidmore calls him a "chameleon" who sided with the evangelicals "once he realized

---

* Transubstantiation is the Catholic belief that the Communion bread and wine literally transform into Christ's body and blood. It was replaced by a service that was purely symbolic of the Last Supper that Jesus had with his disciples before his arrest.

** Justification by faith (or "sola fide") is a key Protestant doctrine that asserts that God's pardon for sinners is received only through faith; believers do not, as with Catholicism, need to do "good works" on earth to be saved.

where Edward's true feelings lay". This charge of "sheer calculated opportunism" is fuelled by the fact that, shortly before his execution by Queen Mary, he declared himself a Catholic in an (unsuccessful) effort to save his skin.[12] Other more supportive scholars, including Barrett L. Beer, point out that Northumberland had long favoured reducing church power and material holdings, and was close to many Protestant reformers. Beer argues that he fully supported Cranmer's ongoing, phased reformation – and what is more, he was

THE IMPACT OF RELIGIOUS REFORMS

There is widespread and continuing disagreement over how successful the Edwardian reformation was. For G.R. Elton, by 1553 "England was almost certainly nearer to being a protestant country than to anything else". Others, such as Eamon Duffy, emphasise the resistance to change and the persistence of old ways. Duffy's view is supported by a host of local studies, which have found evangelical Protestants to be in a tiny minority. The religious changes of the reign were certainly welcomed by a number of reformers, especially in London and the southeast. But in the southwest and the north, many – perhaps most – remained attached to the old religion.

The best way to understand this dissonance is by separating the notions of a "reformation of externals" from the longer process of "changing hearts and minds".[13] Edward's regime achieved radical alterations in appearance and doctrine, many of which lived on in the Elizabethan Church; yet his time on the throne was short and people were not, by and large, converted in such a brief period, as was shown by the speed with which Queen Mary was able to restore Catholic practices. ∎

described by at least one leading evangelical in 1553 as "a diligent promoter of the glory of God".

Conclusion

Though Edward VI's brief years on the throne are traditionally remembered as the "grey" and uninteresting interlude between the glories of Henry VIII's reign and Elizabeth's, they are better represented as "splashed with the crimson of blood spilled in war".[14] These were years of rebellion, inflation, cut-throat politics, war and religious turmoil, a time when "high ideals combined with low opportunism to a marked degree".[15]

Yet despite all their drama, the years 1547 to 1553 don't merit W.R.D. Jones's dramatic label of a period of "crisis". The royal supremacy was upheld; the country retained its independence; it didn't succumb to civil war, largely thanks to Edward's "good" and "bad" protectors. But, as we have seen, these archetypes of the "good" Protector Somerset and the "bad" duke of Northumberland fail under closer scrutiny, revealing fascinating flesh-and-blood figures, men of complex motivation, contradiction and qualification: Somerset the idealist whose ideals were often misconceived and flawed in the execution; Northumberland a "dedicated servant" of the crown who acted with a pragmatic opportunism, but in doing so aroused the resentment of many.[16] Even the tumultuous overthrow of Protector Somerset can be seen less as evidence of instability and more as a sign of a robust system that could effectively replace a failing ruler with a more competent one.

David Loades writes that the true significance of these years lies "less in what happened than in what did not happen", but they did advance two key developments in English history. The first was the Protestant Reformation, whose theological developments would provide a vital reference point into the reign of Elizabeth I and beyond. The second was a critical transformation in the understanding of kingship.

Although Edward indubitably exerted more independence than the "pawn" of traditional history books, his youth nonetheless meant that "sovereign power had to be exercised collaboratively". Edward's ministers assumed far heavier burdens of responsibility than any of their Tudor predecessors. In doing so, they began the transition that would continue through the second half of the 16th century from a state where "the monarch was the kingdom" to a "polity conscious of existence beyond the life of the king".[17] By demonstrating how useful the king's counsel could be in advancing the power of the Tudor crown, the Edward years paved the way for a newly influential privy council and, farther down the line, the parliament-led monarchy of the present day.

ENDNOTES

1. W.K. Jordan. *Edward VI: the threshold of power; the dominance of the Duke of Northumberland* (London: Allen and Unwin, 1970).
    John Dudley was created Viscount Lisle under Henry VIII, then Earl of Warwick on Edward's accession. He took the title Duke of Northumberland only after he became Lord President. For clarity here he is called Northumberland throughout.
2. Christopher Morris
3. John Guy
4. Dale Hoak
5. Dale Hoak
6. J. Clayton
7. Diarmaid MacCulloch
8. Barrett L. Beer
9. *Ibid.*
10. David Loades
11. Barrett L. Beer
12. W.K. Jordan
13. Catherine Davies
14. Jennifer Loach
15. Catherine Davies
16. Barrett L. Beer
17. Stephen Alford

A SHORT CHRONOLOGY

1516 Mary I is born

1533 September 7 Elizabeth I is born

1536 May 30 Henry VIII marries Jane Seymour

1537 October 12 Edward VI is born at Greenwich Palace. Jane Seymour dies 12 days later

1547 January 28 Henry VIII dies. Edward VI is pronounced King. Edward Seymour is named Lord Protector of the Realm until Edward comes of age

1549 March 20 Thomas Seymour is executed for plotting against Edward

1549 France's King Henry II declares war on England

1552 January Edward Seymour is deposed by John Dudley, 1st Earl of Warwick, and executed

1553 July 6 Edward VI dies of tuberculosis leaving the throne to Lady Jane Grey

FURTHER READING

Stephen Alford, *Kingship and Politics in the Reign of Edward VI* (2002)

M.L. Bush, *The government policy of Protector Somerset* (1975)

Nigel Heard, *Edward VI & Mary: a Mid-Tudor Crisis?* (1992)

Dale Hoak, entry on Edward VI in the *Oxford Dictionary of National Biography*

Stephen Lee, *The Mid-Tudors, Edward VI and Mary, 1547-1558* (2006)

Jennifer Loach (eds. George Bernard and Penry Williams), *Edward VI* (1999)

David Loades, J*ohn Dudley, Duke of Northumberland* (1996)

Diarmaid MacCulloch, *Tudor Church Militant: Edward VI and the Protestant Reformation* (2000)

Chris Skidmore, *Edward VI: The Lost King of England* (2007)

Penry Williams, *The Later Tudors, England 1547-1603* (1995)

A SHORT CHRONOLOGY

1516 Mary I is born

1533 September 7 Elizabeth I is born

1536 May 30 Henry VIII marries Jane Seymour

1537 October 12 Edward VI is born at Greenwich Palace. Jane Seymour dies 12 days later

1547 January 28 Henry VIII dies. Edward VI is pronounced King. Edward Seymour is named Lord Protector of the Realm until Edward comes of age

1549 March 20 Thomas Seymour is executed for plotting against Edward

1549 France's King Henry II declares war on England

1552 January Edward Seymour is deposed by John Dudley, 1st Earl of Warwick, and executed

1553 July 6 Edward VI dies of tuberculosis leaving the throne to Lady Jane Grey

FURTHER READING

Stephen Alford, *Kingship and Politics in the Reign of Edward VI* (2002)

M.L. Bush, *The government policy of Protector Somerset* (1975)

Nigel Heard, *Edward VI & Mary: a Mid-Tudor Crisis?* (1992)

Dale Hoak, entry on Edward VI in the *Oxford Dictionary of National Biography*

Stephen Lee, *The Mid-Tudors, Edward VI and Mary, 1547-1558* (2006)

Jennifer Loach (eds. George Bernard and Penry Williams), *Edward VI* (1999)

David Loades, J*ohn Dudley, Duke of Northumberland* (1996)

Diarmaid MacCulloch, *Tudor Church Militant: Edward VI and the Protestant Reformation* (2000)

Chris Skidmore, *Edward VI: The Lost King of England* (2007)

Penry Williams, *The Later Tudors, England 1547-1603* (1995)

Notes

First published in 2016 by
Connell Guides
Artist House
35 Little Russell Street
London WC1A 2HH

10 9 8 7 6 5 4 3 2 1

A CIP catalogue record for this book is available from the British Library.
ISBN 978-1-911187-29-5

Design © Nathan Burton
Written by Anna Neima
Edited by Jolyon Connell

Assistant Editors and typeset by
Paul Woodward & Holly Bruce

www.connellguides.com

Printed and bound by CPI Group (UK) Ltd, Croydon, CR0 4YY